Bilal ibn Rabah
The First Muezzin of Islam

Written and Illustrated by
Shahada Sharelle Abdul Haqq

Published by Tughra Books

335 Clifton Ave., Clifton,

NJ, 07011, USA

www.tughrabooks.com

Bilal ibn Rabah: The First Muezzin of Islam

Written and Illustrated by Shahada Sharelle Abdul Haqq

Development Editing by Khaliff Watkins

ISBN 978-1-59784-941-8

Ebook: 978-1-59784-975-3

Contents

Introduction

When the call to prayer echoes through the masjid or the streets, on TV, or perhaps in the ears of a newly born Muslim baby, a believer immediately remembers Allah – God, the Creator of the heavens and the earth. In this book, I will relay to you how, through God's grace, a humble person born into slavery became a noble companion of the beloved Prophet Muhammad, may the peace and blessings of God be with him. How the Prophet, peace be upon him (pbuh), selected Bilal ibn Rabah to become his trusted friend, treasurer, and the first muezzin (caller to prayer) of Islam is a wondrous story.

Because of the injustices prevalent during pre-Islamic days, God used these events to end belief in the superiority of race, gender, origin or status, as revealed by the verse in the Holy Qur'an:

> O humankind! Surely We have created you from a single (pair of) male and female, and made you into tribes and families so that you may know one another (and so build mutuality and co-operative relationships, not so that you may take pride in your differences of race or social rank, or breed enmities). Surely the noblest, most honorable of you in God's sight is the one best in piety, righteousness, and reverence for God. Surely God is All-Knowing, All-Aware. (49:13)

May the telling that follows in this book move you to learn further about the inspiring life of Bilal and the message it sends to our human family.

Note: There are various reports about who the enslaver of Bilal, may God be pleased with him, was. While it has been widely accepted as Umayyah ibn Halaf, according to other reports he was Abdullah ibn Judan. In this book, we preferred to stick to the preference of the majority.

A note on salutations

Muslims are expected to say salutations of respect and blessings after certain names. Even if not written in the text, we assume our readers will still remember to say these salutations, which are as follows:

* When God's name is mentioned, say:

subhanahu wa ta 'ala (swt): [God] the Most Glorified, the Most High.

* When the Prophet is mentioned, say:

sallalahu alayhi wasallam: May the Peace and Blessings of Allah be with Prophet Muhammad. A shorter version in English is "peace be upon him (pbuh)."

* When any of the Sahaba, or Companions of the Prophet, are mentioned, say:

radhiyallahu anhu/ radhiyallahu anha (ra): May Allah be pleased with him/her.

All human beings were created from a single pair, Adam and Eve. No person is better than another, except in taqwa – being conscious of God. God alone knows a person's true heart.

1. Born into slavery

March 5th, 580 CE. In the Arabian city of Mecca, a black child of African descent was born. His name was Bilal ibn Rabah. Bilal was enslaved. One day, he would become one of the most shining examples of wisdom and spiritual excellence in the history of Islam. His life began around the time that the Messenger of God, our beloved Prophet Muhammad, peace be upon him (pbuh), honored the world with his birth.

Bilal's father, Rabah, came from Abyssinia, an ancient land called Ethiopia in modern times. His mother, Hamamah, was an Abyssinian princess. Both his parents were captured in war and sold as slaves. Traded in the marketplace like property, they were treated as if they weren't really human beings with feelings or rights of their own. Bilal would be born into bondage. He would have no choice but to work for a cruel enslaver named Umayyah ibn Halaf in Mecca.

Rabah and Hamamah had two other children after Bilal, a son named Khalid and a daughter named Ghufayra. At seven or eight years old, Bilal began working exhaustingly without pay. He would herd sheep in Mecca's rugged mountains everyday under the scorching sun. He went hungry most of the time and was always skinny.

Unfortunately, there were people who despised Bilal just because he was enslaved. They called him Ibn Sauda ("son of a black woman"), intending to insult him and his ancestry. Many talked down to him to make themselves feel superior.

2. Bahira the Monk and the Caravan to Damascus

Bilal grew up to become a handsome young man. He was tall, had dark, brown skin and wore a thin beard. He had beautiful African features, sparkling eyes and bushy, kinky hair. Like none other, he was gifted with a strong and musical voice. He possessed exceptional wisdom, intelligence, dignity and self-esteem despite having never received formal schooling.

One day, the young Bilal received news that would change his life forever. He had been selected to join a special caravan on a lengthy journey. Excited for the adventure, Bilal was also sad that he would have to leave his family for a long time. Loaded with valuable wares, the caravan set off for the great markets of Damascus. On the way, Bilal quickly became friends with a young merchant named Abu Bakr al-Siddiq. Bilal admired Abu Bakr's easygoing nature, beautiful voice and recitation of poetry. He didn't treat Bilal poorly just because he was enslaved as other people did. Traveling through the desert felt less tiring thanks to his new companion.

At the town of Busra, in Southern Syria, they pitched tents for the night. If they sold all their goods there, they could buy new ones and return home. If not, they would continue north to Damascus. However, business wasn't the only thing on their minds. During their journey, Abu Bakr experienced a shocking dream. In it, he saw an enormous full moon rising over Mecca and filling every house with light. What could it mean? He had to find someone to help him interpret it.

Abu Bakr learned about a Christian monk named Bahira who lived in a nearby monastery. It was said that the humble man devoted each day to worshiping God and preserving a library of ancient scriptures found nowhere else. Abu Bakr and Bilal decided to visit the wise monk.

Abu Bakr related his dream to Bahira and eagerly awaited his response. "It is a beautiful dream," Bahira said to Abu Bakr, "and may God make it come true." He explained that the dream meant a prophet would emerge from Abu Bakr's community. He would invite humanity to worship God, the Creator of the heav-

ens and earth, and abandon the idols that the Meccans worshiped. A model of good qualities, this messenger would preach
for equal treatment of all lives. Both men were fascinated by
what they heard. Bilal, in particular, found that the experience
had filled him with hope.

3. Newfound Hope

To Bilal, the monk's prophecy was revolutionary. It gave him hope for change in the world. He started to imagine a society built on justice and compassion. "Who knows? Perhaps I'll live to witness those better days?" thought Bilal with anticipation. "Maybe I can throw off the chains of slavery for good!"

Years after the caravan to Syria, Bilal could feel the presence of the coming Prophet in the environment. He was aware of outstanding people in the community who treated the enslaved and the free equally with respect. They reminded him of his own human dignity and spiritual self-worth—and this energized him. Bilal loved going out to the mountains while herding sheep, but it wasn't enough to make him forget his enslavement. His spirit yearned for freedom. His soul grew agitated. He became a seeker of the truth.

One day, Bilal heard good news that warmed his heart. There were whispers that the Prophet was in Mecca spreading wisdom and kindness among the people. He started searching in secret for Muhammad ibn Abdullah (pbuh). Bilal had admired this man's character even before he found out that he was God's Messenger. Like a person in the dark who was hungry for the light, Bilal believed meeting Muhammad (pbuh) would restore his fading hopes.

When the Prophet Muhammad (pbuh) began inviting people to Islam, Mecca's leaders grew increasingly upset. They threatened anyone who went near the Messenger with death. To lower tensions, the Prophet and his close friend Abu Bakr traveled to a cave outside the city. There they worshiped Allah (God) in peace and patiently waited for things to settle down.

4. The Miraculous Encounter

Everyday, Bilal would herd his enslaver's sheep up a mountain. It was the same mountain where he was about to experience something incredible.

Bilal's mind was racing as he climbed the rocky paths. Who was this man named Muhammad everyone in Mecca kept talking about? What exactly did he say to the people he met in secret? Suddenly, a pleasant voice cried out, "Oh shepherd, do you have some milk you can give us?"

Inside a cave stood two middle aged men Bilal did not recognize at first. Their faces were glowing like no one he had ever seen before. They were smiling at him and greeting him like an equal. To most people, he was just a slave, a thing, practically invisible. Bilal's heart skipped a beat. Could one of them be the new prophet he was searching for?

Bilal didn't know it yet, but one of them was the Noble Prophet (pbuh), and this person repeated his request for milk. Suffering from hunger himself, Bilal nervously replied, "No, I do not have any milk I can spare. Only one of the sheep gives milk." He moved closer to the gentlemen and pointed at a beautiful animal. "I get only one bowl a day from this one. It's all I have for food," Bilal continued, hoping not to be asked again.

"Would you sell it to me?" the Prophet inquired. Stunned by the request, Bilal herded his sheep deeper into the cave to get a better look at the strangers. But wait! The second man was his old-time travel companion, Abu Bakr! Happiness and peace poured over Bilal like a wave.

Stepping close to Bilal, the Messenger of God asked, "Could you hand me the cup?" No longer worried about his own hunger but full of awe for the esteem he was feeling in the Proph-

et's presence, Bilal handed it over with joy. God's Messenger milked the sheep, filling the cup to the brim.

This was no ordinary bowl of milk. The Messenger (pbuh) drank and passed the cup to Abu Bakr who drank until he was full then gave it to Bilal. Miraculously, the cup still had milk in it. Bilal drank and drank to his satisfaction. Contented, he asked to sit with the men, and they both agreed.

Every word he heard brought him delight. He felt his mind expanding and his spirit soaring with each jewel of guidance, knowledge and enlightenment. As Bilal repeated passages from the Qur'an that the Prophet (pbuh) had recited to him, he knew that he was sitting with no ordinary individual. Moved by the Messenger's beautiful qualities, Bilal felt a divine light entering his heart. Finally, he said the shahada, declaring his new faith, and became a Muslim. "I bear witness there is no god but Allah (God)," he said out loud in the cave. "And I bear witness that Muhammad (pbuh) is the servant and Messenger of Allah (God)."

As evening fell, Bilal gathered his flock and raced back to his enslaver's home. Umayyah ibn Khalaf noticed the animals appeared well-fed. "It seems you have found them a good pasture?" he inquired.

"Yes, I have found fertile pastures," Bilal replied, trying to not raise suspicion.

From now on, Bilal would look forward to herding his sheep to the cave where the Messenger of God stayed. He went every day to listen to newly-revealed verses of the Qur'an and gain wisdom from the Prophet's teachings. Each evening he left feeling more hopeful than the day before.

5. *Thinking Like a Free Man*

The nonbelievers, such as a devious man named Abu Jahl, started to slowly notice changes in Mecca. One day, he stopped by the house of Bilal's enslaver, Umayyah ibn Khalaf, and asked why his sheep looked so well-fed and not sickly like they had a few days ago. "You're right! I can't explain it," Umayyah said. Abu Jahl suspected that the Messenger of God was somehow involved. He was furious that Bilal could be meeting Muhammad (pbuh) somewhere outside the city. Umayyah sensed that something bad was about to happen. He ordered Bilal to stop going to those new and mysteriously fertile pastures.

Thankfully, God the All-Knowing protected the Prophet (pbuh) by causing him to leave the cave. Back in Mecca, he continued to guide people. He kept teaching that the enslaved and their masters were equals as humans. This enraged many of the city's elites. The last thing they wanted was for the enslaved to become spiritually emancipated. They thought that Islam's message of equality was dangerous. Bilal's master decided to take all those he enslaved out of Mecca, except Bilal and a few others.

While Bilal was technically still enslaved, he was spiritually attaining great peace. Bilal turned his heart away from his oppressors' abuse and opened it wide to God. He was beginning to feel that he could never again bow to an idol even if his enslaver commanded it.

Mecca's elite made a show of worshiping idols. In reality, the objects they carved from stone were often reflections of their own selfish desires. Some got rich off of the money pilgrims spent during their visit in Mecca. Arrogant chiefs

boasted their deities were better than those of other tribes. The powerful used the idols as an excuse for cruelty, oppression and war. To Bilal, belief in only one God, the Creator of the universe, meant a path to justice, unity and peace.

Bilal was now thinking like a free man. He had come to believe that an eternal life in the Hereafter was much more important than this temporary world. The Hereafter was where he would find everlasting beauty and splendor beyond imagination.

Bilal soon told his loving family about his newfound religion. He described the extraordinary encounter with God's Messenger in the cave, relating word for word what he had learned. His relatives were deeply inspired but also worried. Their enslavers could kill them if they chose to follow this new prophet. "Give us time to think this over," Bilal's mother, Hamamah, said.

Hamamah remembered how priests had warned against idols. They foretold of a messenger who would be sent by God to all humanity. She had kept her own Christian beliefs hidden, even from her children, out of fear for her family's safety. But what she was hearing from Bilal seemed to prove what her former priests had taught. Not much later, she embraced Islam, as well.

6. Abandoning the Idols

As God's Messenger (pbuh) advised, Bilal told no one outside his family about his new faith. Still, he cherished being near the Ka'ba, God's Sacred House, and visited it whenever he could. One day, he left home at the crack of dawn and made straight for the Ka'ba when nobody else should have been there. He looked around, making sure he was alone. Bilal did the tawaf (walking prayerfully in a circle around the Ka'ba). Then, he offered more prayers and sat down to contemplate the spiritual aspects of his inner world.

Intense emotion tore through his soul. It was as if all of the injustice, oppression, and suffering that he had endured throughout his life had flashed before him in a single instance. He stood, glaring at the idols around the Ka'ba. A desire to avenge a lifetime of wrongs done to him, often in the name of those idols, burned inside him. He started to scream at the top of his lungs. A slave, emancipated in spirit, he released his anger over the oppression his body still suffered and directed it toward the largest idol. "May those who worship you be ruined!" he cried.

"Did you just curse our gods and us who worship them?!" a man hollered. Lost in himself, Bilal had failed to notice the Meccans sitting on the other side of the Ka'ba. Outraged, they edged toward him. Unable to speak anything other than the truth Bilal said, "Yes. I cursed them." He ran for his life.

With those in hot pursuit, Bilal had nowhere to turn but the living quarters of his enslaver's residence. His master, Umayyah ibn Khalaf, emerged to face the crowd. "Are you a heretic!?" a man shouted at him.

"How can you blame such a thing on me? I've always held to our ways. I would sacrifice one hundred camels to Lat and Uzza," Umayyah ibn Khalaf replied.

"Well, your black slave just denounced our idols," people from the crowd snapped back. "He cursed them and us for worshipping them. Then he tried to get away!"

Umayyah summoned his steward. "I thought I told you to take all the slaves out of the city!" Find this slave and bring him to me!" he raged. After a while, the steward dragged Bilal from his hiding place, hitting him again and again. The enslaver tossed Bilal to the angry throng and stepped back into his house.

A group of Meccan leaders, including Abu Jahl, took Bilal into custody. However, Umayyah ibn Khalaf, seeing Bilal's defiance as a personal insult, eventually took charge of his punishment. Seething with pride, he wanted to make an example of Bilal. Mecca's slave trade was at stake. "Without submissive slaves, who would do the work? Who would cater to the city's elite?" Umayyah thought.

This new religion of Islam would undo all that had been done to make some people feel superior to others. It taught that all human beings were created equal. This was a dangerous idea. There was no way Umayyah could stand for it.

7. Bilal's Torture

Mecca's rulers feared that the swelling number of new Muslims would produce an uprising. They had to act fast. They wanted to make Bilal regret the day he embraced Islam and strike fear into the hearts of all the enslaved. The so-called nobles quickly gave Umayyah ibn Khalaf approval to bind Bilal and drag him through the city's streets at high noon under the scorching desert sun.

People spilled out from their homes. Some took pity on Bilal. Others laughed. Even children taunted the poor man, imitating the adults. Bilal hardly noticed the crowd; physical pain left him almost unconscious.

Umayyah ibn Khalaf's men were exhausted as they dragged Bilal in the terrible heat. They had to take turns resting when they placed the Prophet's companion on the burning sand and tied his hands and feet to stakes in the ground. "Deny Muhammad!" Umayyah yelled, kicking Bilal's barely responsive body. "Deny Muhammad or face a dire end!"

Bilal was unable to answer. "I will be a laughing stock if I cannot produce a change in this slave," Umayyah thought, exploding with rage. He grabbed a whip and lashed Bilal until he completely blacked out.

A free person in his heart, Bilal would not respond in the way his abusers wanted. Nothing could make him renounce his faith. All he wanted from life was to be a good person.

Every day, the stonehearted Umayyah tortured Bilal in different ways. Bilal's only response was to utter, "Ahad, ahad. (One, one God alone)." Soon, Umayyah's patience ran out. He wondered if he should kill Bilal on the spot. "That will only make us look weak," said Abu Jahl, only concerned about their prideful image.

On a frighteningly hot day, they put Bilal in an armored suit and shackled him to the ground under the boiling sun. "I will never associate partners to God," said Bilal, "even if it means my death." His torturers removed the armor, and Umayyah ordered them to place a giant boulder on his bare chest. As several men struggled to lift the heavy stone, they were amazed by Bilal's endurance.

Bilal wasn't the only one who faced brutal persecution. Other enslaved people experienced such harrowing violence. One of them, a man named Ammar ibn Yasir would look back on those horrible days. "They tortured us to make us say what they wanted, even if it was just with our tongues, not with our hearts," he'd recall. But Bilal would only say what his heart told him: "One God! God is one!"

8. Patience and Relief

The Prophet Muhammad (pbuh) visited the oppressed, encouraging them to hold steadfast. He would spend his days finding ways to buy the enslaved from their persecutors and set them free. One day, the Prophet's companion Abu Bakr Siddiq witnessed Bilal tied to the ground. A boulder was crushing his chest. Horrified, Abu Bakr turned to Umayyah.

"Just how long are you going to torture this man?"

"Am I supposed to just let him go after all this effort?" Umayyah replied.

Abu Bakr responded to Umayyah with wisdom. "If you torture him to death, you'll turn him into a hero, a martyr," said Abu Bakr. "And the people will direct their anger toward you." Umayyah pondered his words. "I am prepared to buy him from you," Abu Bakr continued.

Umayyah started haggling over the price. At last, Abu Bakr offered five ounces of gold, an amount so high the enslaver could not say no. Umayyah handed Bilal over to Abu Bakr.

Abu Bakr removed Bilal's bindings and had the heavy rock lifted off his chest. Dispassionately, Umayyah said, "What if I had refused to sell him to you at that price?"

"Then I would have paid even a hundred ounces," Abu Bakr answered, helping Bilal to his feet.

Bilal turned to Abu Bakr and said, "If you have bought me for yourself, keep me. But if you've bought me for God's sake, let me go."

"You are free, Bilal," responded Abu Bakr.

Bilal stayed in Abu Bakr's home while his wounds healed. Abu Bakr was now a wealthy merchant. He remembered the time they first met on the caravan to Syria.

Abu Bakr began teaching Bilal to read and write and employed this noble companion of the Prophet to tend his store. Bilal was almost forty years old.

In old times, ink had to be prepared from scratch. One day, Bilal was making ink when Abu Bakr kissed his hand. Bilal pulled his hand away, quickly, as this gesture was an expression of extreme reverence that no one had ever shown him.

"I have heard from the Messenger of God that the ink of a scholar's pen is holier than the blood of a martyr," Abu Bakr explained. After living for so long being seen as less than human, a loving calm overtook Bilal's soul. It was as it says in the Holy Qur'an (2:153), "Surely God is with the persevering and the patient."

9. The First Muezzin

Prophet Muhammad (pbuh) advised some of his companions to migrate from Mecca to Medina. Bilal was among them. When they arrived, Medina's inhabitants, rich and poor, embraced the immigrants and provided for them as if they were their siblings.

Five times each day, the Messenger of God (pbuh) instructed Bilal to go to Medina's streets and marketplaces and invite people to worship. Bilal greeted the Muslims saying, "as-salat, as-salat (the prayer, the prayer)" or "as-salat aj-jamii'atun (prayer brings the people together)." However, this became impractical as the Muslim population grew. With construction on the mosque progressing, the Prophet (pbuh) turned to his companions for advice. What would be the best way to gather everyone to prayer? Some suggested hoisting a flag. Others preferred blowing a horn. "Sounding a horn is the Jewish custom," replied the Messenger of God.

"We should light a fire, so everyone will see it," one person called out.

"That's the Zoroastrians' practice. We can use a hand-bell," someone else said.

"The Christians use a bell," remarked another person.

Days later, the Prophet's companion Abdullah ibn Zayd rushed up to the Messenger.

"Oh, Messenger of God!" he began. "I was between sleep and wakefulness when, suddenly, a man dressed in green and carrying a bell approached me." Flushed with excitement, Abdullah continued telling his story. "I asked him, 'Would you sell me your bell? We will call the people to prayer with it.' And he said, 'Shall I teach you something better? Face the qibla and say:

Allahu akbar, Allahu akbar – God is great, God is great!

Allahu akbar, Allahu akbar – God is great, God is great!

Ashhadu an la ilaha illa'llah – I bear witness that there is none worthy of worship except God!

Ashhadu an la ilaha illa'llah – I bear witness that there is none worthy of worship except God!

Ashhadu anna Muhammada'r-Rasulullah – I bear witness that Muhammad is the Messenger of God!

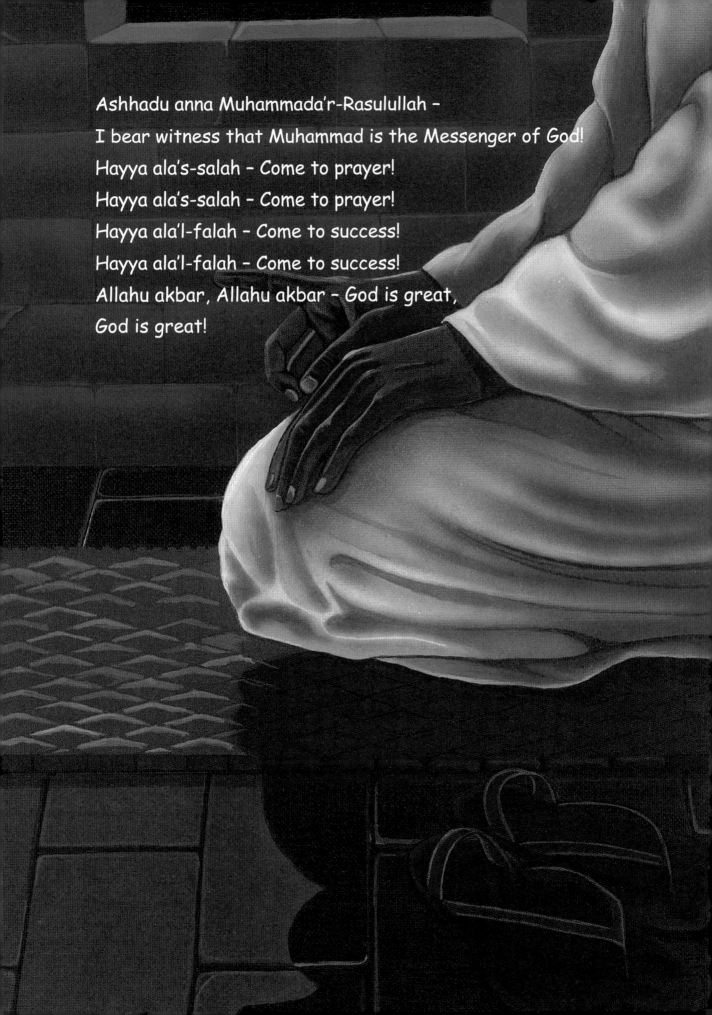

Ashhadu anna Muhammada'r-Rasulullah –
I bear witness that Muhammad is the Messenger of God!
Hayya ala's-salah – Come to prayer!
Hayya ala's-salah – Come to prayer!
Hayya ala'l-falah – Come to success!
Hayya ala'l-falah – Come to success!
Allahu akbar, Allahu akbar – God is great,
God is great!

Another companion, Umar, revealed that he too had experienced a similar dream. "God be praised that this fact has been confirmed," said God's Messenger (pbuh). "Now go to Bilal and convey what was said in your dream. Let him make the call to prayer, as his voice is more far-reaching."

Once enslaved and now free, Bilal ibn Rabah recited the first ever adhan (call to prayer). He would recite it from the roof of the house of a woman named Nawar bint Malik. He did this until the Prophet's mosque was completed with a place made for him high on top to call the adhan. In addition to becoming the first muezzin, Bilal also received the honor of serving as the Messenger's secretary of the treasury. He was in charge of distributing alms to the poor.

Bilal's spiritual station was so exalted that proof of it extended beyond this world. One day, the Messenger of God (pbuh) approached Bilal with a question. It was soon after the Prophet (pbuh) had traveled to the heavens and back in a single night, what is called the great Night Journey (Al Isra' wal Mi'raj).

"What great virtue do you possess, Bilal?" asked God's Messenger (pbuh). "For wherever I went in the heavens I could hear your footsteps."

"Oh Messenger, I have no virtue," Bilal humbly replied. "Except that, throughout my life, I have tried not to sin. And if I do, I immediately make wudu (ablutions), perform two raka'at (units of prayer) and ask God for forgiveness and mercy. And I always try to keep my wudu to remain in a state of ritual purity."

10. The Battle of Badr

Mecca's rulers, the leaders among the tribe of Quraysh, had tortured the enslaved. They had made the lives of the Meccan people miserable. And they still hated the Muslims.

The Meccans had already driven the Muslims from their homeland to Medina, an eight-day journey away. All the believers wanted was to live in peace. However, a Meccan army was marching in their direction.

The Muslims were still hurting from when the Meccans had stolen their property. Now, they had to face their persecutors in combat. The Battle of Badr occurred on the 17th of Ramadan in a valley surrounded by mountains. The Meccans were about 1,000 men with 100 horses and 170 camels. The Muslims of Medina numbered about 300 with only two horses and 70 camels. Unseen were the archangels Jibril (Gabriel) and Mika'il (Michael), with 3,000 angels assembled to support the believers.

The Meccans thought they were superior in number and weapons. They believed they would easily wipe out the Muslims, once and for all, and capture everything they owned. Strong faith in God is what held the believers together.

The Prophet Muhammad (pbuh) prayed to God. "O Allah, the Almighty; this is the Quraysh. They have come with all their arrogance and boastfulness, trying to discredit me," the Messenger implored. "My Lord, if this Muslim band should perish today, no one will remain to worship You."

Battle commenced. The Prophet could see the angels in front of the believers. Their horses' feet did not even touch the ground. In the middle of the fighting, the Messenger took a handful of sand. He blew it at the Meccans, and, in moments, a sandstorm formed. It scattered the Quraysh and sent them fleeing.

The Muslims treated the captured Meccans humanely. Anyone among them who could teach ten believers to read and write was set free. The Prophet (pbuh) called on Bilal to distribute the spoils of war. In this way, Bilal served as the first treasurer of the Muslim ummah (community). Whenever any poor or needy person came to the Prophet (pbuh), he would send them to Bilal to receive food or clothing.

11. Marriage

One day, Bilal received the joy of a visit from his brother, Khalid ibn Rabah.

"I have asked a noble woman's hand in marriage," said his brother. "I told them I am the brother of Bilal ibn Rabah, the companion of the Prophet of God (pbuh). They said if I brought you to them as proof that you are my brother, they would accept my marriage offer." Khalid had not told the woman and her relatives about his own family's past in slavery. Bilal did not like this. He thought that his brother should have told the whole truth about himself.

Bilal and his brother went to the family. Bilal was an honest person. "I am Bilal ibn Rabah, and this is my brother," he told them. In Islam, both sides should know one another with their strengths and weaknesses before deciding to marry. Disappointed with his brother for not mentioning that his family had once been enslaved, Bilal said, "He has a temper and is not always of the best character. However, if you wish to accept him in marriage to the lady, then go ahead."

Honored to have Bilal in their home and moved by his honesty, the family agreed to Khalid and their daughter getting married.

As for Bilal, perhaps God's Messenger (pbuh) would help him find a spouse when the opportunity came? After all, the Prophet was close to him and knew his character well.

One day, members of the Banu Bukayr tribe approached the Prophet (pbuh). A woman from their community named Hind was looking to marry. God's Messenger (pbuh) suggested Bilal as a potential husband for the lady. However, the idea of their daughter marrying a freed slave was unthinkable to them. The Messenger (pbuh) asked, "Where do you stand regarding Bilal?" They gave no answer. The tribesmen made a second and third visit to find Hind a suitor. Finally, the Prophet (pbuh) said, "Where do you stand regarding one of the people of paradise?" He meant Bilal, of course.

The Banu Bukayr leaders gave their blessing to the marriage of Hind al-Khawlani and Bilal ibn Rabah. However, their belief in the superiority of lineage was a centuries-old prejudice that had to be uprooted. When Bilal went to meet Hind's family, her brothers rejected him. In response to her family's wrongdoing, Hind said, "How can you prevent me from marrying Bilal ibn Rabah despite the recommendation of God's Messenger?" Realizing that they had made a mistake, they apologized for their un-Islamic behavior and proceeded to make arrangements for the wedding. Hind and Bilal would live together in happiness and serenity, with their mutual love, good character and the guidance of the Prophet (pbuh) to help them through life's challenges.

Years later, after God's Messenger (pbuh) had passed away, Bilal could no longer bear to live in Medina. Everything there reminded him of the man he so dearly loved. He decided to settle in Damascus, and there his beloved wife Hind would also pass away. Grieving doubly, Bilal let some time pass before looking to marry again. When he did, he introduced himself and his friend Abu Ruwayha, who was also looking for a wife, to the tribe of Banu Layth.

"I am Bilal, and this is my brother in Islam," he said. "We were astray, and God guided us. We were enslaved, and God freed us. We were impoverished, and God gave us wealth. Should you consent to our marrying your daughters, all praise is to God. If you should turn us away, all power and strength is with God." The Banu Layth accepted their offers to wed into the tribe. Bilal had no children from his marriages.

12. Leaving This World Behind

The passing of the Prophet Muhammad (pbuh), one of the most exalted human beings to ever live, caused Bilal great sadness. Bilal had been the seventh person to accept Islam. He had persevered by the Messenger's side throughout the period of the Qur'an's revelation. Now, the city of Medina and everything in it reminded him of the man he had loved with all his heart.

While reciting the adhan (call to prayer), Bilal would choke up with tears when he came to the name Muhammad (pbuh). He could no longer serve as the community's muezzin (the caller to prayer). Bilal had gone from being enslaved and persecuted to receiving the envoys of kings and chiefs on behalf of God's Messenger. Grief humbled him once again. He felt an empty loneliness in his soul.

One day, Umar, the second caliph and leader of the Muslims after the Prophet, visited Damascus. The people asked Umar if Bilal would once again call the adhan. Bilal stood up and lifted his voice. It was the first time since the passing of the beloved Prophet Muhammad (pbuh) that he was reciting the call to prayer in public. Remembering good times with the Messenger of God in Medina, all the companions of the Prophet (pbuh) wept.

Following his emigration to Damascus, Syria in the eighteenth or twentieth year after the Hijrah (migration from Mecca to Medina), Bilal fell seriously ill. Realizing he was about to breathe his last breath, his wife cried out in sorrow. Bilal lovingly tried to console her. "It's a time for joy," he said. "Tomorrow I shall meet the beloved Messenger of God (pbuh) and his companions!"

May God be well pleased with all the great men and women who dedicated their lives to serving God on the path of Islam.

We honor Bilal with every adhan called throughout the world. Let us remember that one's color, lineage, economic status, social rank, tribe or position in this world does not set them above anyone else. It is sincere consciousness of God and righteous conduct that elevate a person in their faith. Those who believe in one God and who do good deeds are the ones who are elevated.

The Adhan

Allahu akbar, Allahu akbar

God is great, God is great!

Allahu akbar, Allahu akbar

God is great, God is great!

Ashhadu an la ilaha illa'llah – I bear witness that there is none worthy of worship except God!

Ashhadu an la ilaha illa'llah – I bear witness that there is none worthy of worship except God!

Ashhadu anna Muhammada'r-Rasulullah

I bear witness that Muhammad is the Messenger of God!

Ashhadu anna Muhammada'r-Rasulullah – I bear witness that Muhammad is the Messenger of God!

Hayya ala's-salah – Come to prayer!

Hayya ala's-salah – Come to prayer!

Hayya ala'l-falah – Come to happiness!

Hayya ala'l-falah – Come to happiness!

Allahu akbar, Allahu akbar

God is great, God is great!

References

The Holy Qur'an: English Translation of the Meanings and Commentary, published by Mushaf Al-Madinah An-Nabawiyah.

Bilal al-Habashi. 2017. by Hilal Kara and Abdullah Kara, NJ: Tughra Books

Bilal ibn Rabah: From Darkness into Light. 1992. Translated by Sara Saleem, Ta-Ha Publishers, UK.

Selected Hadith

Abu Dawud Salat, 28: Ibn al-Athir, usd al Ghaba, 2953

Shami, Subul al-Huda 3:254

Ibn Sa'd, Tabaqat, 7:385

Ibn Manzur, Mukhtasar, 13:39 Sahar, Bilal Mu'adhdhn ar Rasul,8

Baladhuri, Ansab al-Ashraf, 1:207-208   Ibn Manzur. Mukhtasar, 5:203

Ibn Sa'd, Tabaqat 3:232 Baladhuri, Ansab al-Ashraf 1:210

Baladhuri, Ansab al-Ashraf, 1:211

Shami, Subul al-Huda, 3:254

Abu Dawud, Salat, 28: Ibn al-Athir, Usd al-Ghaba, 29531